The Things That Mattered

A Retired Teacher's Look Back on
Fifteen Strategies That Made a Significant Difference in Her
Classroom

by
Sue Zapf

Printed in the United States of America
ISBN: 978-1793019547

First Printing: February 2019
Independently published

Cover design by Zannie Carlson

Email Sue: thethingsthatmattered@gmail.com

CONTENTS

INTRODUCTION

This book is not a typical book on education. It is not about the research I have read or that I have conducted. It is, however, about the journey of a teacher who began teaching in the secondary schools at twenty-one years of age, continued to teach for thirty-five more years and loved almost every minute of it. Once she got the hang of it.

That teacher — me — graduated from a small college in northern Minnesota in the late 1970's with a degree in English education and a minor in speech and theatre. In the world in which I grew up, I could only see myself as a teacher, a nurse, or a wife. Because I was not fond of blood and because I was not dating anyone, I chose the teacher option.

After graduation, my first job was at a high school in southeastern Minnesota, and while it was mainly a positive experience, nothing had really prepared me for the reality of teaching. I did not know how to respond when a student said, "No, I won't." I did not know what to say when a student — after learning she had earned a failing grade — told me she would be calling her "lawyer dad" and would have me out of teaching by the end of the day. And I did not know what to think when an eighth grader told me that he knew neither the alphabet nor his home address. In spite of that, I loved teaching — most of the time.

At the end of my first two years, Minnesota was experiencing all sorts of educational budget cuts, and many teachers throughout the state, including me, were laid off. With a limited number of jobs available in Minnesota, I applied for a job in Las Vegas, Nevada. I was surprised to find myself hired as a junior high teacher there. For the next three years, I was considered an effective teacher, but the long hours and daily practice of teaching began to burn me out. At the end of the third year, I felt I could no longer put so much of my time, energy, and heart into teaching, and I simply left the profession — with the intention of NEVER again returning to the classroom.

For that reason, I packed up my life and enrolled in a three month travel school in St. Louis, Missouri. There I learned about ticketing, making reservations, operating travel reward systems, and even bringing planes to the gate. Three months later I was hired by the now-defunct Midway Airlines in Chicago, and I began my new career as an airline reservationist. Of course, this work was nothing like I had ever done before, and I loved it. I never had to take work home, I did not start working each day until noon, and I was able to fly at a very low cost around the country. However, by the end of that winter, I was not loving it as much. Each day I would go to work, but it was not with anticipation or passion; it had become simply a job that needed to be done.

In April of that year, I knew I needed to make a change; I needed a job where I felt I was making a significant difference in the lives of others. I decided, very deliberately this time, that

I wanted to return to teaching. So, with a new attitude and a renewed spirit, I applied for teaching positions once again and was hired in a suburb of Minneapolis/St. Paul as a high school English teacher. Even I was surprised I was back in the classroom! However, I knew I had to do things differently because this time I intended to stay in the profession.

I remained at that same Minnesota high school for fifteen years until I moved within the same district to an area learning center where my co-teacher, John, and I taught at-risk eighth and ninth graders for an additional fifteen years in a program now called COMPASS (as in a "place for new direction"). It was in that environment with those students where I learned the most about the things that really matter in education, the things that turn teaching from a science into an art. Simply stated, I learned that many of the things that "count" in education just cannot be counted.

While politicians continue to argue about educational policy, testing, and standards, I offer here what that experience taught me about what makes things "click" in the classroom. While some will argue education is all about the content, I will argue that educating students is about teaching the content while enveloping the students in a caring, inviting, and challenging environment in which they not only grow in knowledge and skills but where they also grow as people. As most of us have experienced, many of the directives we hear from politicians, administrators, and our communities are directly related to the content or to the data or to the assessments. Very little of it is directed to the environment where all of that learning and assessing is supposed to take place. However, it is in that space where the "magic happens." And if we do not give consideration to that space, we will, unfortunately, continue to lose many students along the way.

One of those students may have been Oliver,* who became our student in my thirty-second year of teaching, and with whom I faced some of my greatest challenges as a teacher. He came to us as a seventh grader — although our classroom was typically for eighth and ninth graders, on rare occasions we took seventh graders when other options were not good options for them — and he was completely helpless as a learner. Whenever anything was presented to him, his only response was "I'm confused" in a slightly whiny voice. Shortly after he joined us, we discussed special education options, but because his test scores were so low, we knew he would not qualify. We even spoke to his mom about talking with his doctor about a possible neurological disorder. He could not plot points on a number line, his handwriting was illegible, his writing was confusing, he scored poorly on all tests and quizzes, and he was completely disorganized. These patterns continued for most of his seventh-grade year, and although he was a very gentle and kind student, he remained an enigma to our team for almost his entire first year.

As a COMPASS student, Oliver "lived" the strategies I offer in the following pages for three years. While the changes in Oliver did not happen quickly — not quickly at all — they did happen for him in life-changing ways, and those same strategies have the ability to transform *your* daily practice into something almost magical as well.

*Not his real name

CHAPTER ONE

Strive to Be Intentionally Inviting

While taking a course early in my second-time-around-teaching-career, I was assigned to read a book that completely transformed my life as a teacher. That book was *Inviting School Success: A Self-Concept Approach to Teaching and Learning* (Purkey & Novak, 1984). For the first time, I realized how much influence I had in the students' attitudes, their successes and failures, and in how they perceived school. From that point on, the ideas in that book were indelibly imprinted on my brain and in my heart, and they became an integral part of my classroom culture until I retired.

In their book, Purkey and Novak (1984) explain how a teacher's actions fall into one of four categories (pp. 17-20):

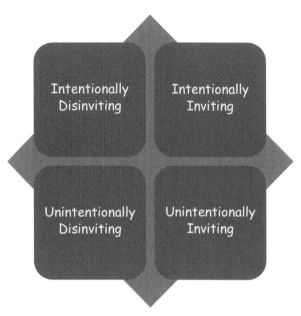

Intentionally Disinviting

"You'll never amount to anything."
"You're nothing like your older sister."
"I've already explained that twice. You need to be a better listener."

An *intentionally disinviting* teacher is one who says things or acts in a way that intimidates a student, basically putting a wall between herself and the students. Perhaps, she might say to a class, "I only gave one A last semester" or "If you are late, I will lock the door" or "If you don't have a pencil, you will have to go without one." In this type of classroom, students generally respond from a place of fear.

Unintentionally Disinviting

"Your older brother did a great job in my class."
A sterile-looking classroom
Interrupting others

An *unintentionally disinviting* teacher is one who sends disinviting messages, but they are not sent with the intention of creating fear or intimidation in the student. In fact, sometimes they are just a natural reaction to a situation. Often, I have been unintentionally disinviting when I have spoken to a colleague or a student while I continued to type on my keyboard. Or when a student has asked a question, I know I have sighed loudly or have given him "that teacher look." I remember a time when a student asked to go to her locker, and I heard my "Why didn't you bring your book with you?" tone of voice attached to the word "Yes."

Unintentionally Inviting

"How are you doing today?"
(Teacher says it because that's how they treat others.)
Music in classroom
(Teacher plays it because he/she likes it.)
"I appreciate your help."
(Teacher naturally expresses gratitude.)

The third group of teachers that Purkey and Novak (1984) go on to describe is an *unintentionally inviting* teacher. She is a natural-born teacher who can be very effective but has never really thought about all the classroom dynamics and, therefore, cannot always purposefully repeat or create success. For the most part, the day-to-day operation of the classroom goes well, but when a bad day occurs, she has difficulty determining what changes need to be made. The authors compare the unintentionally inviting teacher to barnstorming airplane pilots (or stunt pilots) in the 1920's.

> *As long as they stayed close to the ground and the weather was clear, so they could follow the highways and railroad tracks, they did fine. However, when the weather turned ugly or night fell, they became disoriented and got lost. In difficult situations they lacked consistency in direction (pp. 18-19).*

In the same way, as long as all is going well in the classroom, the unintentionally inviting teacher does well, but when less than favorable occurrences happen, they often are not sure how to handle each situation.

Intentionally Inviting

"I don't know the answer to that, but let's figure it out."
Music in classroom to set tone and mood
Knowing students' names and pronouncing them correctly

According to Purkey and Novak (1984), the ultimate goal to which all teachers should strive is to be an *intentionally inviting* teacher. These teachers are proactive in everything they do — from their relationships with students and parents to their lessons to their conversations with others. They *invite* students to be successful in their classrooms many times a day in a wide variety of ways. This is the teacher who thanks a student for coming when he arrives to class three minutes late, this is the teacher who answers the same question five different ways until the student understands it, and this is the teacher who notices the new hair color, the funky nail polish, the new nose ring, and the fun-colored shoes — even if those shoes look as though they have been "borrowed" from a bowling alley. Again, Purkey and Novak (1984) compare those teachers in this category to pilots — modern jet pilots.

> *Thanks to their knowledge, they can 'fly on instruments' if need be — around or even over dangerous weather fronts. It is this ability to chart and maintain a dependable 'flight pattern' that makes the difference between success or failure as a teacher (p. 20).*

Richard was a student who lived with his two brothers and his dad in a small apartment. Although he usually was on time for school, now and then he was late — sometimes as much as two or three hours late. One day he arrived about 11:00 in the morning, and I thanked him for coming — as I always did — and told him we were glad he had arrived. Later that day I privately asked him why he had been late, and this was his story: His brothers had been up late celebrating their birthdays, got drunk, and he ended up sleeping in a closet so he could get some rest. When he woke up, he was almost two hours late for school, and he thought coming to school late would be better than not coming at all. Thanking him instead of punishing him for arriving late made it more likely he would repeat that choice another time.

Be aware that being *intentionally inviting* can involve everything you are and do as a teacher.

It's what your classroom looks like.

It's your tone of voice and facial expression when a student asks to borrow a pencil for the third day in a row.

It's the color of pen you use to write comments on their papers.

It's pronouncing students' names correctly.

It's greeting students in the hall as you pass by them on your way to the office.

It's the positive energy you bring to your classroom every day.

In fact, it can be as easy as asking students "What questions do you have?" which invites questions, instead of asking, "Do you have any questions?" which is often met with shaking heads indicating *no*.

While I would love to be able to say that I was always an *intentionally inviting* teacher, that is far from the truth. Early in my career, I spent a great deal of time in the intentionally disinviting quadrant as I tried to follow the "Don't smile until Thanksgiving" guideline. Then, through trial and lots of error, I moved into the *unintentionally inviting* teacher quadrant and had some success there. However, it was not until I became *intentionally inviting* on a more regular and purposeful basis that I really could sense a positive shift in my abilities as a teacher, and I felt myself being in full control of the "*aircraft.*"

CHAPTER TWO

It's All About the Relationships

*"They won't care how much you know until
they know how much you care."*

This quote is very true, and it should come as no surprise. Currently, many businesses and organizations — from healthcare systems to ad agencies to religious bodies — market themselves with the message that they value the relationships with their clients, their employees, and their members above anything else. Why should education be any different?

However, based on what you hear from the media, politicians, legislative bodies, and sometimes administrators, education is all about standards and accountability. Yes, the content is important, and, yes, accountability is important, but for some students, if you do not have a positive relationship with them, they are not going to learn anything that is put in front of them. On the other hand, there are many students who will "just do it" no matter the circumstances. There will always be those students. You can intimidate them, you can disrespect them, you can ignore them, and they will succeed in spite of that. But there will also always be some students who will just tune you out — and be happy to take the failing grade. Many students who struggle in school are those students. If you are not interested in knowing who they are, they are not interested in doing anything for you. Many have failed so often that getting one more F will not faze them a bit. At least if they fail, you, the teacher, will "get off their backs," and they will not have to listen to you or your lectures anymore.

Early in my career I told a group of boys if they did not put their names on the paper they shared, they would get a 0/10 on a group assignment. Guess what? Their names were not on papers, and I felt I had to follow-through on my threat. Of course, some of those students (the ones with whom I did not have strong relationships) took that information home to their parents, who were livid about the zero. It cut me deeply when I was told by their parents in a meeting with an administrator present that my teaching "was less than mediocre" and that I should no long be a teacher. That meeting was the low point of my career, and I never wanted to repeat it.

It took me a long time to realize it, but the situation was not really about the zero at all; it was about me using the power I had as a teacher to follow through on the directions I gave. I now think that if I had had a positive relationship with those young men, they likely would have accepted the consequences much more readily. And although it has taken me a long time to get to this place, I now consider that situation to have been one of the best lessons of my career.

The relationship aspect of teaching is based on the "first the heart, then the head" philosophy. It is about understanding that not everything you teach students is going to stick with them. However, the way you treat them will. Recently, on a local talk radio station, people were calling in to tell about their favorite teachers. In the ten calls received, nine of them stated their favorite teachers cared about them, taught them to be resilient, made them feel valued, and/or believed in them. Only one mentioned the ability of the teacher to make the content interesting or easy to understand. The relationship, rather than the content, was key.

The bottom line is that every person on this planet — the A student, the F student, the CEO of a major corporation, the owner of a small business, the drug addict, the stay-at-home mom or dad, the celebrity, the insurance salesperson, the shy, red-headed adolescent — wants to matter to someone. They want their voices to be heard and their time on this planet to be recognized by someone. As a teacher, you are in the incredible position of being that person to so many kids. Consider that a gift, and embrace it.

Another great thing about building relationships is that it does not take time away from the curriculum. It is just "how you do business." It is how you treat the students, how you speak to them, how you respond to them, how you listen to them, how you interact with them. It is you being *intentionally inviting.* Often, when I observed teachers in situations where they were humiliating or threatening or embarrassing students, I wondered how the teachers would feel if that was the way their administrators treated them. Enough said . . .

CHAPTER THREE

Everyone Has a Bag

Teaching students the "everyone has a bag" concept is a great use of your time because it works really well. Basically, you explain to the students that each one of us carries a figurative "bag" on our backs, which is filled with all of our life experiences as well as our reactions to them. In one student's bag might be a parents' divorce, a trip to Boston, and a disabled sibling. In another's there is an angry parent, poverty, and an affinity for animals. Someone else might be carrying around the experience of being harassed in school or on the bus, a close relationship with a grandparent, and an ill sibling. On a daily basis all of us choose to share or not to share those things in our bags. My co-teacher, John, and I began each year by sharing some things in our bags. Because John and I both have gay relatives and friends, we shared that with the students, explaining that when we heard the word *gay* as in "That's gay," we felt the word was being used in a derogatory way, and we did not appreciate it. I also shared my experience in the mainstream schools when I often ignored students who said, "That's retarded," simply because I was not sure how to respond. Well, I ignored it until a tenth grader came up to me after class one day and said, "I really don't like it when kids say, 'That's retarded' because I have a retarded brother." I felt like I was an inch tall and vowed I would never ignore that word again. By sharing both of these stories from our bags, we rarely heard the words *gay* or *retarded* in our classroom. If we did, an "I'm sorry" quickly followed, or if a new student said those words, he was promptly corrected by his peers saying, "We don't say that word in here."

Also, as we shared from our own bags — the good and the bad — it deepened the relationships we had with our students as they often felt more comfortable sharing parts of themselves with us. In a sense, they became aware that we, too, had both likes and dislikes, strengths and weaknesses, good and bad experiences, just like everyone else in the world.

We also explained that because there are many things in our bags we choose not to share, other people may not always understand us. For example, a teacher may yell at a student and not understand when that student or possibly even another student completely shuts down because he is unaware of the difficult home situation where yelling is the norm.

In addition, we used this strategy when students felt that others might be receiving special privileges. We would respond by saying "It's in her bag," which meant that it was private to that student and something she needed. Students often wondered why Samantha got to sit in the hall and Josh did not, why Philip had been gone for so many days, and why Anthony did not have to turn in an assignment on the day it was due. We simply explained, "It's in his/her bag," and the conversation always ended. Early on, we explained to students that they probably did not know everything in other students' bags — and we as teachers were more likely aware of it — so nothing could be judged as fair or unfair without knowing the entire picture, which would often lead us into a "fair is not always equal" discussion.

In fact, one year it was decided by our administration that one of our students would be best served if he did not attend school in the building for the final two weeks of the school year. After about three days, students began to ask, "Where is Peter? Why isn't he here? Will he be back before the end of the year?" "It's in his bag," was our response, and we never heard another word about it.

CHAPTER FOUR

Codeswitching

Codeswitching is something that many people learn naturally at a very young age, but some people actually need to be taught the concept. According to All Kinds of Minds, codeswitching is the students' ability to "adjust their language in response to the current audience" (2018, para. 2). In our classroom, we expanded that definition to also include nonverbal language, such as facial expressions, tone of voice, and dress. When I first introduced the word to the students, I asked them if they spoke the same way with their grandparents as they did with their friends; immediately, they understood the concept. Or when I asked them if they would wear the same type of clothes to the mall as they would to a funeral, they easily recognized that we change our "code" depending upon the situation. And they certainly knew that the "codes" we use are not the same when we text a message as when we write an academic paper.

By making sure all kids understand this idea, it allows you to manage the language in your classroom very easily — as long as you have a good relationship with your students. If a student says an inappropriate word in class, the only word you need to say to them is "Codeswitch" in a very non-emotional manner.

One of my favorite stories is about a student who had a very colorful vocabulary. One day something happened in class to which she responded, "Oh, s---!" Immediately, she covered her mouth and said, "I have to learn to codeswitch!" We didn't have to say anything more. Another year, a young man showed up to class wearing much nicer clothes than were typical for him. I asked him what the occasion was, and he commented, "I have a job interview, and I thought I had better codeswitch."

And, of course, if a student says "- - - - you!" directly to a staff member or another student, you do not respond with "Codeswitch." That is a respect issue and needs to be dealt with very differently.

CHAPTER FIVE

Life Can Get in the Way of Learning

Years ago, Chloe came to school one wintry day, still in her pajamas, just because it was a warm place. During the night the police had thrown flashbangs through the windows of her home because they believed her father was suicidal. Her home was cold, and the only reason she came to school that day was to stay warm. No matter how brilliant my lesson was that day, it was likely that Chloe did not learn it. She had too many other things on her mind. While this may be an extreme example, life often gets in the way of learning for kids. A pet may die, parents may argue, harassing words may be said, or a grandparent may get sick. The student's world has been turned upside down, and she just wants to get through the day. No matter how creative, exciting, and engaging your semicolon, Civil War, or photosynthesis lessons are, it is unlikely those students are going to learn them.

As teachers we just need to understand that in the same way we are not always on the top of our game every day, neither are our students. Sometimes life gets in the way, and we need to understand that on some days learning how to use the semicolon needs to be secondary.

CHAPTER SIX

Choose Your Attitude

While most of us have heard this over and over, how many of us really *choose* our attitude? Most of the time we let our attitude dictate our day — often at the expense of the relationships we have with our students. For the last twenty-five years of my career, I tried to make a conscious decision each day to choose the attitude I shared with both my colleagues and my students. Yes, I might have had a headache; yes, there might have been stresses at home; yes, life got in the way of work in the same way it does for students. But each day I tried to remember that I was going to make a difference — either positive or negative — in the life of each student every day. So, I consciously chose to make that difference a positive one. That meant greeting all students when they entered the room, asking, "What's up?" to the student who seemed a little off, or noticing the new purple hair on the normally orange-haired student. Those seemingly little things changed the energy in the classroom. When you change the energy, your students respond more favorably, they work harder for you, they engage more willingly, and ultimately, they learn more.

Often, teachers complain about a negative class or negative students. While I certainly have had my share of them myself, they were much easier to deal with when I worked to live the words of Ghandi, "Be the change you wish to see in the world," or my slightly revised version, "Be the change you wish to see in your classroom." You can be that change with a change in attitude.

CHAPTER SEVEN

Some Kids Struggle with "Doing School"

For many of us who are teachers, "doing school" — the daily tasks like keeping materials organized, remembering to complete homework, turning in assignments, and taking the right supplies to get through a school day — came naturally, and as a result, we cannot imagine it should be difficult for anyone else. One of the most common denominators among our at-risk students was that they simply lacked the "doing school" skill. We had students who were extremely bright, but their inability to find materials, to have a pencil and paper, to remember to turn in their work, or to find what they needed before or during class resulted in a lot of failure for them.

Several years ago, a young man who scored very high on both his reading and math standardized tests joined the COMPASS program because he was failing all of his eighth-grade mainstream classes. It wasn't that he didn't care, it wasn't that he was lazy, he just had a great deal of trouble being organized, and he was consistently penalized for it. If you had opened his binder, you would have seen that he not only had his hole-punched papers in the wrong sections, he also had them backwards and upside down as well! Rarely could he find anything he needed for school. Initially, John or I would sit down with him and organize his binder, showing him how it should look, and gradually we turned that responsibility over to him. It was a very slow process, but about mid-year, he admitted that he saw value in staying organized, and he began to make the effort to keep his materials in order. His binder was never perfect, but it had improved a great deal over the course of the year. Perhaps, more importantly, he saw that we recognized an area of growth for him, and as a team, we were willing to help him develop a skill rather than punish him for the lack of it.

CHAPTER EIGHT

Every Student Is a Slot Machine

While I would love to take credit for creating this metaphor, I cannot. I heard it at a seminar years ago, but it is one that I thought about daily. Basically, the idea is that in the same way you put coins into a slot machine, you put tokens — asking kids questions, listening to them, showing them patience, allowing them to explain themselves, giving them opportunities for success, or any acts of kindness — into each student. As you probably know, most often when you put coins into a slot machine, you do not see the jackpot because the payoff is hours or days or weeks or months or even years down the road. In the same way, when you are kind to kids, when you are patient with them, when they feel as those you understand them, you are putting "coins" into them as people. While you may never see the "jackpot" — their high school or college graduations, their success in their jobs or as parents, their boost in self-confidence — if you never put those coins "into" them, there will never be a jackpot at all.

Of course, we have not seen the jackpot in all of our students, but we have been fortunate to experience some payoffs:

We saw Zoey, in her first few months with us, spend several hours of her day under her desk in an effort to avoid those around her, recruited by the military as a result of her excellent test scores; she served in Kuwait for nine months.

We saw Cooper, who joined us as an angry young man who was failing all of his classes, attend a university in Wisconsin to study fashion design, even going to London one semester to pursue that dream.

We saw Layla who attended college to become a social studies teacher.

We saw Lily who now has three kids and loves being a mom.

We saw Claire, a teenage mom, earn her high school diploma.

We watched Maya receive a $500 scholarship to attend post-secondary school, where she would earn a degree in ultrasound technology.

Sometimes the jackpots even came in the form of thank-yous:

"Thank you for believing in me when I didn't believe in myself."

"Thank you for your kindness."

"Thank you for showing me how to 'do school.'"

"Thanks for understanding when my life was one big mess."

Yes, the jackpots do come, but they can only come after the "tokens" have been put into their lives.

CHAPTER NINE

Own-its and Fix-its

One of the challenges of teaching is trying to help students understand that when they blame others or situations for their grades, their poor score on a test, their incomplete assignment, their having a poor relationship with a teacher, they are really giving away their power. While John and I, too, struggled with how to address this issue with our students, we had more success once we explained to students about Own-its and Fix-its, based on the recommendation of our school psychologist, who used it with her own children.

By "owning" a behavior or a grade, students also empower themselves to fix it. If a student blames a teacher for a poor end-of-quarter grade with comments like "She doesn't like me" or "He wouldn't let me do extra-credit" or "She won't help me," that student is transferring the blame — and the power — to someone else, and nothing about the grade can be changed. However, when the student owns it and realizes that he did not put forth as much effort as he could have, that he missed several assignments, that she did not ask for help when the assignments were not clear, things can improve as the improvement now lies in the hands of the student which is where the change — or fix — can happen. When this concept is explained to students in Own-it and Fix-it terms, they understand the entire school process much more clearly. There is much less blaming and a lot more doing.

CHAPTER TEN

Teaching and Learning Are Not the Same

How many times have we all heard or said, "I can't do this or that because I have to teach all of the standards"? Yes, most teachers have more standards than they have time to teach. And for some reason we think that if we just cover them all — quickly, if necessary — we have done our job. Unfortunately, that is NOT the case. If our students are not learning what we teach, then why have we spent classroom time teaching it? Often, we lecture and test, lecture some more, ask some questions, do an activity and test, but have students really gained anything in that process? They may have been able to regurgitate what you have covered in class, but in two weeks, has anything stuck? What have they really learned?

What we cannot do is equate <u>teaching</u> and <u>learning</u>. Think about your own students. Think of something you have taught them. They took the test. Some passed and some failed. What did you do? For many of you, you probably went on to the next unit, needing to get all of those standards covered. But that is not what this job is about. If the students have not learned it, then your job is not done. A failing grade simply means there is more work to do. Yes, I know that is extremely difficult, but that is the truth. Poor grades support the bell curve, but does the bell curve support learning for all students?

CHAPTER ELEVEN

The Power of Optimism

As teachers, it is important for us to show our students the possibilities, show them what they can accomplish, and show them what their lives can become. Some students love school. They do their homework, they participate in extra-curricular activities, they enjoy the process of learning. They see themselves going to middle school, high school, and on to some sort of post-secondary training. However, there are also many students who would prefer to do anything except attend school. They do not do their homework, they hate being in class, they are not interested in the social aspect, and they do not see a bright future for themselves. In fact, I have had several students ask me, "Why do I need school? I will be in jail or dead by the time I'm thirty."

To secondary students, we explained that for some of them, school might simply be seen as a series of hoops that they have to jump through, hoops that they may prefer to avoid. Hoops might include having to write one more paper or take one more test or do an assignment they might consider busywork. Sometimes we had to remind them that "life beyond school" does not usually look like school. They will not be expected to do well in every subject from math to art to music to science every day. However, if they are willing to jump through the hoops, they *will* earn their diploma, and that will be their ticket to *choice* — choice of post-secondary options, choice of career, choice of career location — where they will be able to follow their passions and strengths. On the other hand, if they are unwilling to jump through those hoops, those options decrease dramatically.

Think about it. I would suspect that most of you reading this book are teaching the subject you are good at — and not the one you nearly failed. Keep in mind that kids only know school and its environment — where they are often expected to be good at everything. We need to remind them to look toward the future — a future that they can create — and it is likely that future will not look like school.

CHAPTER TWELVE

Teach Students About Their Brains

So often, kids rate themselves on how smart they think they are or how dumb they think they are. Typically, it is thought that the "smart" ones sail through school, and the "dumb" ones struggle. For years, John and I taught our students that all of our brains are different, that we all have strengths and weaknesses, and that our lives and our learning are affected by how we take care of our brains. In addition, we taught our students the work of Carol Dweck, as explained in her book *Mindset: The New Psychology of Success (2008),* that intelligence is not fixed, and learning is really all about the effort. School — and life outside of school — is not about how quickly things can be done or just completing tasks; rather, it is about doing your best by putting forth your best effort. It is about the learning, not about the grade.

For many students, this is NEW thinking. For most of the students in COMPASS, they stopped putting forth any effort months before they arrived at our school. They did not do homework, they did not do classroom assignments, they slept in class, they chose to fail — and then they often blamed their failures on a force outside of themselves.

I will always remember Dominic who had struggled in school since third or fourth grade. He was having a particularly hard time with math, and he stayed after school to work one-on-one with his math teacher. After about forty-five minutes of work, I walked into the classroom, and he said with a big smile on his face, "This is finally making sense. I have finally grown some math dendrites!"

It is time to show all of your students that their potential resides within themselves — and teaching them about the brain can do just that.

CHAPTER THIRTEEN

The Habits of Mind

If you are not familiar with *Learning and Leading with Habits of Mind: 16 Essential Characteristics for Success* (Costa & Kallick, 2008), it is definitely worth a read. In the chapter "Describing the Habits of Mind" (Costa, 2008), Costa describes the sixteen habits that are consistently observed in successful people — students and adults. The sixteen characteristics range from *persistence* to *striving for accuracy and precision* to *responding with wonderment and awe*. The coolest part of the list and what you want to share with students is that none of the sixteen traits has anything to do with one's intelligence, power, or economic status. For some students, your explanation of that might be the first time they think that success can be a part of their futures. Unfortunately, too often, students hear or perceive these words: "You are too dumb," or "Why can't you be smart like your brother/sister?" or "That was a stupid move." And although those words may not actually be said directly to them, some kids get a sense that only those adults with intelligence or power or money are going to be the successful ones, and because they often perceive themselves as unintelligent, powerless, and/or poor, they will never have the skills to become successful. The Habits of Mind can change all that.

To help students better understand these concepts, John and I would discuss each of the skills, observe the skills in others (often through videos) and try to practice the skills within the classroom setting. For example, the concept of *persistence* can be taught through crossword puzzles or sudukos — or any activity where students might want to give up when it gets challenging. After introducing *striving for accuracy and precision*, we no longer told students to check their work. Rather, we would tell them to "strive for accuracy and precision." As the students began to understand this concept, they no longer tried to write well just to meet our expectations; they were trying to be more accurate and precise with their writing. While most often the changes in the students occur subtly, they definitely do occur.

CHAPTER FOURTEEN

Black and White Versus Shades of Gray

I have to confess that if the daily acts of teaching were black and white — if this happens, do that, or if that happens, do this — my life as a teacher would have been much simpler, although likely more stressful. But in that world, all kids would have to come to us alike. Yet, too often, we want to treat kids like that. If Evan or Sadie or Autumn says a swear word, we send them to the office. If Naomi or Cora or Joseph has an outburst, we put them into the hall — and we think all will be better the next day. I am sorry to tell you, it does not work that way. While all kids need to be treated fairly, sometimes that means they are treated differently, and those differences are usually a result of what is "in their bags."

In order to do that, John and I always took the time to explain to our students at the year's beginning the meaning of "fair is not always equal." When students are familiar with that concept before emotions get involved, they are much more likely to understand and accept it.

CHAPTER FIFTEEN

Each Day...

Each day commit to being a better teacher than you were the day before. Often, we take notice of the work of our colleagues. We will notice those who work hard, but we also notice those who appear to hardly work, who come in late, and who have a bad attitude. I, too, have been guilty of all of these judgments.

We can also be guilty of being intimidated by those teachers who seem to have more skills than we do — or at least different sets of skills. Rather than feeling inferior, look to them for opportunities to learn. Talk with them, observe them, ask them questions, and listen to them. Be open to what they can offer you. You do not want to become them, nor do you want to compete with them. You simply want to better yourself. Accept their help and their advice. You are all on the same team!

The reality is that there will always be a teacher who has more skills than you do, and there will always be a teacher who has fewer skills than you. Avoid putting your energy into judging or competing with them; rather, place your energy into being a better teacher than you were the previous day — and your teaching career will be much less frustrating and much more enjoyable.

FINAL THOUGHTS

So now I am hearing some of you say: "Yeah, this sounds good, but does it really make a difference? And I have so many standards, how am I possibly going to fit any of this into the day?" Well, the good news is that, while there does need to be some upfront conversation and teaching early in the school year, it then all becomes just the way you manage your classroom. It is how you talk to students, how you plan your lessons, how you manage your day. There really is no extra time expended; in fact, you will spend less time dealing with classroom issues because they will become less frequent.

And I also hear some of you saying, "Well, that might work in your alternative learning center, but I am in the mainstream classroom, and I just don't have time for that." Keep in mind that I, too, taught in a mainstream classroom for twenty years, and I began using some of these methods in my seventh year. The bottom line is that you need to make it a priority. Yes, you will need to take some time to have some discussions with the students, to introduce them to the terms and concepts, and to make them very aware of your expectations. Maybe the first year you only introduce two of the strategies. Add another the following year but use only those that resonate with you. Leave the rest behind. However, if you do find value in them, allow them to unfold in a way that works for you and then share your experiences with your colleagues. There is a great deal of power in having an entire staff — including support staff — on the same page when working with students. And keep in mind that only about five of the fifteen strategies require student understanding; the others are about *you* and *your* attitudes, perceptions, and behaviors.

So, getting back to the question, "Does any of this make a difference?" I am going to let Oliver, the young man I introduced early in the book, answer that for me. He was a tenth grader in the alternative learning center's high school program when in response to the prompt, "Describe how your time in COMPASS impacted you as a student and as a person," he wrote the following words, and with his permission, I share them here:

> *Before Compass, my life was one which followed a set repetitive course. This course was one that was simplest for my life, one where I didn't need to expose myself to the world. The school I went to was pretty average, but I was one of the unlucky few who some wanted to tear down. My grades slipped down to F's and D's, and they rarely ever climbed to C's. I got sick often, but the bullying also made me want to stay home more than ever. My assignments kept delving further into this abyss of hopelessness, making it so I could never catch up. I was told to kill myself almost weekly by these bullies. Eventually, I started to feel suicidal thoughts as well. I never thought about actually doing it, but I always wondered how it would feel to have the pain, as well as everything else, just disappear. My parents eventually got a divorce, due to my father's behavior, and the emotional*

strain pushed me further back. I felt isolated, and I only ever wanted to be by myself, even pulling myself away from my own family. I just wanted to lock my feelings inside of me.

My mother was concerned about my condition and searched for an alternative. We started home-schooling, but I grew incompetent studying by myself, as my mother had to continue working to support our household, including our lives. She had heard about the Compass program from one of her associates at work, and we gave it a shot. For a majority of the first year, I remained in the same mindset. I blocked almost everything out, to the point that I can't remember practically anything from the classes that I "zoned out." Sue and John, and probably many more of the staff, held many meetings about what to do about my behaviors, about me not wanting to do anything.

I would always get out of my work by saying 'I don't know' or 'I'm confused.' Eventually, Sue pushed me in the right direction by saying "Yes, you do," and with that simple statement, I was stunned. Never had someone actually forced me to do my work, but it definitely got me going. Eventually, my mindset began to slowly change, and my life grew more positive. The second year I was there, I had already changed drastically. I had grown more independent, more competent, and above all, happy. I didn't drown my mind with sorrows from the past any more. Instead, I began to grow more creative. My grades jumped back up to A's, B's and C's, and I grew to enjoy the classes themselves, along with the great teachers I had to guide me. The third year, I grew even more competent, with my grades reaching mostly A's and B's. I learned that I had developed a knack for writing, and I learned to love doing it.

I am now a student who gets mostly A's and A-'s. I am constantly praised for my good behavior, and I've grown to love the world around me. I still feel badly about my past, but my experiences at Compass definitely outweigh the setbacks which allowed me to get there. For Compass, I would have gone through it all again. Compass turned a lost cause like me into an academic success. I wouldn't have made any progress without the help of my teachers: Sue and John. They were the ones who kept pushing me forward, even when I myself had given up. Even greater, they were the ones who got me to keep moving forward. I want to give the both of them the credit they deserve, but before that, my gratitude.

Compass changed my life entirely. I led one of gloom and anguish, to one of positivity and hope. I hope to grow into the person that everybody wants me to be when I'm grown, and I want to thank Sue and John for giving me the best Compass experience I could have ever asked for.

So, while educational policy, testing, and standards continue to be reviewed, debated, and revised, the educational system is actually much more than that. The attitude, the relationships, and how you go about doing what you do *are* things that matter, often resulting in that which cannot be measured nor counted in typical ways. What can be counted, however, is one life-changing experience for a young man named Oliver, and it is one John and I will always consider one of our greatest jackpots.

REFERENCES

All Kinds of Minds. (2018). Adjusting language for different audiences. Retrieved from http://www.allkindsofminds.org/utilizing-verbal-abilities-to-relate-to-others-adjusting-language-for-different-audiences

Costa, A. L. (2008). *Describing the habits of mind.* In A.L. Costa and B. Kallick (Eds.), *Learning and leading with habits of mind: 16 essential characteristics for success. (pp. 15-41)*. Alexandria, VA: Association for Supervision and Curriculum Development.

Dweck, C. S. (2008). *Mindset: The new psychology of success.* New York: Ballantine Books.

Kallick, B. O., & Costa, A. L. (Eds.). (2008). *Learning and leading with habits of mind: 16 essential characteristics for success.* Alexandria, VA: Association for Supervision and Curriculum Development.

Purkey, W. W., & Novak, J. M. (1984). *Inviting school success*: A *self-concept approach to teaching and learning.* Belmont, CA: Wadsworth Publishing.

ACKNOWLEDGMENTS

First, thank you to Dan, my husband, for your support of my career and the writing of this book. You knew I loved what I did, and you supported me on every step of this journey. So very grateful!

My niece, Heidi, who encouraged me to follow this process through to the end, even when I wasn't sure what to do next. And to Lori, another niece and currently a secondary teacher. I appreciated hearing your perspective — often on our drives to and from the lake — as we discussed the book's details.

My friends and fellow educators, Pat, Karin, John, Cindy, and Barb, who read the early drafts and believed the content was worthy of print. And, Pat, your "English teacher skills" are still strong in *your* retirement. Thank you!

My colleague, Michelle, who introduced us to Own-its and Fix-its. Thanks for sharing your wisdom!

My co-teacher, John, who shared the last fifteen years of this journey with me. Thank you for being willing to listen to "another one of my crazy ideas" and especially for being willing to try them in the classroom — even when you were not convinced they were good ideas. We were a great team!

Ken, the principal who hired me upon my return to the classroom. You believed in me more than I did, which set me on a career path I could not have imagined. I will be forever grateful.

Faith and Cliff, two principals in the alternative setting, who encouraged us to implement the "crazy creative" approaches in the classroom. Thank you for empowering us.

To Zannie, my editor, who brought this book to life. For a couple of years, it was just a pile of papers on which my thoughts were written, and you were instrumental in helping me move forward with it. I am so grateful I was sitting right behind you that day at a writers' workshop because you were the catalyst for transforming that pile of papers into a real book. My sincerest gratitude! And thanks, too, for the great cover as it truly captures the energy of the book.

And finally, to all the Olivers, Laylas, Samanthas, and Dominics who passed through my classroom door. I am grateful to each of you for the laughs and for the lessons. May you always remember, "You are worthy, and you are loved!"

ABOUT THE AUTHOR

A Minnesota native, Sue Zapf taught Language Arts in secondary public schools for over 30 years. For the first half of her career, she was a teacher in mainstream junior and senior high schools. For the last fifteen years, she taught in an alternative setting, working with at-risk students. While she was teaching, she developed a teacher-mentoring program for teachers new to her building, and she also co-created COMPASS, the program which became her greatest passion.

Sue also co-authored a chapter in the Association for Supervision and Curriculum Development's (ASCD) book *A Better Beginning – Supporting and Mentoring New Teachers (1999)*. In addition, she published "Reaching the Fragile Student" in ACSD's *Educational Leadership* magazine (September 2008).

In 2004, she was a finalist for the Minnesota Teacher of the Year.

She retired in 2015.

Not a fan of cold weather, Sue, along with her husband, Dan, now spend the winters in Arizona and the summers at their cabin in west central Minnesota.

Made in the USA
Columbia, SC
15 April 2019